SISKIYOU
609 S. GOLD ST.
YREKA, CA 96097

811 POL   63623

POLISAR, BARRY
PECULIAR ZOO

DATE DUE	BORROWER'S NAME	ROOM NUMBER

Siskiyou County
Office of Education Library
609 South Gold Street
Yreka, CA 96097

63623

SISKIYOU CO. SUPT. SCHOOLS
LIBRARY
808 S. GOLD ST.

Peculiar Zoo

by Barry Louis Polisar
illustrations by David Clark

The Okapi

The okapi seems self-conscious
Here in his jungle patch;
His legs look like a zebra's
But his body doesn't match.

The Caiman

The caiman is a crocodile,
Related to the gator.
With such a family tree as that
I would not irritate her.

She lives beside the water,
She's scaly underneath.
And no one dares to scold her
When she doesn't brush her teeth.

The Numbat

A numbat is an animal with
An interesting feature;
It has more teeth than any
Other zoologic creature.

And yet despite so many teeth,
It's dining style is crude,
For when the numbat sits to eat,
It never chews its food.

The Frilled Lizard of Australia

The frilled lizard walks about
In the outback, puffing out.
When attacked, he fills with air
And warns intruders to beware.

Ballooning red and blue and yellow,
He's a frightful looking fellow.
With mouth agape, he puffs up quick
And hisses, but it's just a trick.

He's really harmless, not so tough;
His act is nothing but a bluff.
Attackers back off in dismay,
Then he turns and runs away.

The Dik-Dik and the DoDo

The dik-dik and the dodo
Went to their favorite spot.
The dik-dik came back afterwards;
The dodo still has not.

The Goosefish

The goosefish swims beneath the sea;
I hope it won't swim under me.

The Proboscis Monkey

The proboscis monkey has a nose
That's certainly endowed
Proportionately larger than
A nose should be allowed.

The Manatee

Most have cuts upon their backs
And scars upon their sides
From motorboat propellors that
Have sliced into their hides.

Endangering these sea cows
As only humans can,
Makes me wonder who's evolved:
The manatee or man.

The Solenodon

When attacked, it sticks its head
Deep inside a hole.
Its instinct is to hide itself
Which takes a tragic toll.

Even the oddest Ostrich,
Despite what has been said,
Will never sink to such a depth
As burying its head.

Because it is a foolish thing
To leave oneself so bare,
I think it is no wonder
That solenodons are rare.

The Three-Banded Armadillo

The banded armadillo
Looks like an armored knight
Protected by its plated shell
And suited for a fight.

Yet when an armadillo
Gets in a fearful brawl,
It doesn't stand its ground and fight;
It rolls up in a ball.

Although it looks aggressive,
The banded armadillo
Fights danger by becoming
A passive, hard-shelled pillow.

The Warthog

Warthogs are not graceful,
I state with much regret.
They do not make good dancers.
They cannot pirouette.

You'll never see one take a bow
At some recital hall,
And yet the other warthogs
Still love them, warts and all.

The Naked Mole Rat

Naked mole rat.
Eek! Imagine that!

Emperor Penguins

Huddled close together
Against the snow and sleet,
Penguins at the Pole
Pool their body heat.

They gather in a circle,
Steadfast, disciplined,
Turning toward the center,
Fighting off the wind,

Sharing warmth and comfort
On cold and icy floes,
Balancing their future
Gently, on their toes.

The Yakow

A yakow is a creature
That's half yak and half cow.
I don't know which half is which
Or if they'll moo or plow.

Does the yakow have a hump?
Or just a bump upon its back?
How can a cow be so endowed?
Which part's cow? Which part's yak?

The Zebu

Read a book on animals
And surely you will find
A picture of the zebra
With stripes on its behind.

I wonder if the zebu,
Who often is excluded,
Ever feels depressed or sad
When he is not included.

Caiman: A member of the alligator family, residing in Central and South America. Some caimans grow to five feet in length. Others such as the black caiman grow to fifteen feet and are noted for their ability to change colors quickly.

Dik-Dik: A small African antelope, named for the sound the female makes when in danger.

Dodo: An extinct, flightless bird.

Emperor Penguin: Residing in Antarctica, emperor penguins have adapted well to cold climates; several thousand birds will huddle together nesting on the ice floes. Male penguins incubate the eggs of the female, carrying them on their feet, tucked under the folds of their belly skin.

Frilled Lizard: An Australian reptile, the frilled lizard is a fast runner. When attacked, it hisses and unfurls its umbrella-like collar in an attempt to frighten predators.

Goosefish: A fish with a mouth as wide as its body and filled with teeth. It is also known as the monkfish.

Manatee: A sea cow, native to the warm springs of Florida. When manatees venture out into the rivers in search of food they are often killed or maimed by passing motor-boats.

Naked Mole Rat: A small, furless mammal that is about three inches long with a gray-pink body, skinny legs and buck teeth. It lives in underground societies similar to a bee or ant colony, serving a queen. Virtually blind, naked mole rats hardly ever come above ground but will defend their colony--and their queen--from intruders.

Numbat: Also known as the banded anteater, and native to Australia, the numbat has more teeth than any other animal, but swallows its food, mostly ants and other insects, whole.

Okapi: An African mammal, related to the giraffe but smaller. The okapi has leg markings resembling a zebra. It is a solitary animal and hides amidst the thick jungle growth.

Proboscis Monkey: A monkey native to Borneo in Southeast Asia. The male proboscis has a long, flexible nose that hangs down over his mouth and occasionally touches his chin. When eating, the proboscis monkey must move his nose out of his way with one hand, while he feeds with the other. When excited, his nose turns red and swells.

Solenodon: A near-extinct, rat-like animal of Cuba and Haiti with a large snout and a hairless tail. When attacked, it buries its head in a hole. Contrary to popular belief, the ostrich does not bury its head.

Three-Banded Armadillo: This armadillo, native to South America, is related to its American cousin, the nine-banded armadillo. It can literally roll itself into a tight ball and protect itself from predators.

Warthog: A wild pig of Africa with large tusks and warts on its face.

Yakow: A cross breed of the Tibetan yak and common cow.

Zebu: A domesticated Asian cow with large horns that it uses to protect itself from predators.

PECULIAR ZOO © 1993 by Barry Louis Polisar
Illustrations © 1993 by David Clark
Published by Rainbow Morning Music
2121 Fairland Road, Silver Spring, MD 20904
ISBN 0-938663-14-3 First Edition

63623